Delicious Strangeness:
A Pocket Guide to Magical
Realism

Stephanie Barbé Hammer

Spout Hill Press

First Edition

April 2018

Spout Hill Press
San Dimas, CA

Book design by Ann Brantingham

ISBN 10: 1986107817
ISBN 13: 978-1986107815

Delicious Strangeness:
A Pocket Guide to Magical Realism

Stephanie Barbé Hammer

Praise for Stephanie Barbé Hammer

Like magical realism itself, Stephanie Barbé Hammer has the miraculous ability to teach the genre in a grounded, easy-to-understand way. Her directions are clear and concise; her love and exuberance for the art form, absolutely infectious.

--Rich Ferguson, LA performance poet/novelist, author of *New Jersey Me* (Rare Bird Books)

A grimoire of magical tactics by a riveting teller of enchanted tales. Pick it up, and be prepared to be transformed. . . "

--Robert F. Gross, poet, director, and frog prince

for my writing students

Acknowledgments

I could not have thought up let alone written *Delicious Strangeness* without the inspiration of John Brantingham whose *Gift of Form* craft book launched the charcoal series. John was the first person to suggest that I try my hand at writing a craft book on Magical Realism, and I thank him so much for that idea and for his support. Elder Zamora, the Spout Hill publisher became my valued developmental editor and he made crucial suggestions for how to expand chapters and deepen explanations of how Magical Realism works. Artist Ann Brantingham designed the book you hold in your hands and served as copy-editor. Thank you Elder and Ann! I'd like to thank Erin Martinsen for permission to reprint her brilliant Proppian analysis of Disney's *Cinderella* and Anne Galloway for her permission to reprint part of her wonderful surrealist games web page. In addition, I extend my admiration to the Magical Realism practitioners featured in this book, particularly Ryka Aoki, Aimee Bender, Heather Fowler, and Stacey Levine. The prompts and exercises offered in this book riff on the concept of the specific, strange assignment as developed by author Bruce Holland Rogers, and the exercises were refined in classes offered at the Mount SAC Writers Weekend, Hugo House, Seattle, and the Inlandia Institute, Riverside. I want to thank Christine Texeira of Hugo House and Cati Porter of Inlandia for their support of this work. Finally, I want to extend my appreciation and love to my friends and family members for their special touch of genius weirdness that makes me want to write and teach Magical Realism: Larry Behrendt, Lillian Behrendt, Jo Scott-Coe, Robert Gross, Andrea Grossman, Robert Murphy, Hilary Henry Neff, Liz Newstat, Erika Suderburg, Susan Waters, my Whidbey Island MFA writing kinfolk, and my writing communities in Los Angeles, the San Gabriel Valley, Riverside, Claremont, Coupeville, Langley, and Seattle. Thanks for helping me keep it unreal.

Contents

Introduction: How I Fell in Love with
    Magical Realism   11

Try this Little Writing Exercise   18

1. What IS Magical Realism?   21

2. How Does Magical Realism Work?   23

3. Plot and Character: Understanding and Using
    the Fairy Tale Model   28

4. Style, Part 1: Languaging Magically   40

5. Style, Part 2: Who's Talking? A Note on Point
    of View   45

6. Style, Part 3: Go Big -- Multiple Points of View
    AND Time   55

7. Other Story Reboots to Try   61

8. Magical Realism and Non-Happy Endings   65

9. And Now the Big Question: Why
    Magical Realism?   74

10. Books and Articles Mentioned in this Book   79

11. Bonus Chapter: Mind-Boggling Games
    and Six More Prompts   83

Appendix A: How to Freewrite   91

Appendix B: Lingo List   97

Postscript: Before We Go...   99

Introduction: How I fell in love with Magical Realism

I have always loved fairy tales and stories with magic in them. When I had to stop reading them in favor of grown up novels, encountering literature often made me very sad. It was so "real" and often kind of boring! On the other hand, fantasy novels like the Narnia books and the *Fellowship of the Ring*, made me miss my every day experiences. Where were the taxicabs in Mordor? Why couldn't Aslan just fix World War II, dismantle all the nuclear warheads and then make everyone a milkshake? *[12] Why couldn't Gandalf be Dean of my university? Or sell me a really great car? Or make my daughter do her homework?

In other words, why did fantasy worlds have to be so – distant? Why couldn't the real world have more magical elements in it?

This is exactly the divide that Magical Realism seeks to bridge.

I had my first official encounter with Magical Realism when I took a yearlong creative writing course

---

* It's no coincidence that my favorite of the Narnia books is the one with a street lamp and a crazy bachelor uncle and an evil queen who breaks through the worlds-barrier and goes berserk in downtown London. The street lamp gets thrown into Narnia and stays there.... And that's my favorite image of the series.

at UCLA Extension with Magical Realist author Aimee Bender. In this class, we read books and talked about them and then used those conversations as jumping off points to create our own short stories or novels.

The class reading list included five very strange books. I will describe them briefly so that you can get a feeling for the many ways that Magical Realism can express itself, and the different sorts of forms MR can take:

1. *The Bald Soprano* is a one act stage play by French-speaking Romanian author Eugene Ionesco about an evening at home with Monsieur and Madame Smith and their friends Monsieur and Madame Martin, along with a housemaid named Mary and her boyfriend the fire-chief. The play was performed in 1950, and features comical, ridiculous discussions. During one such conversation Monsieur Martin and Madame Martin exchange banal pleasantries like "where do you live?" until they eventually realize – to their astonishment – that they are married to each other. Another famous conversation narrates the physical health and general condition of an extended family who all go by the name of Bobby Watson.

I've made this play sound very boring, but it isn't. It's really funny and thought provoking.

I loved that this play could be – in the words of Jerry Seinfeld – "a show about nothing" and I loved its silliness – a silliness that truthfully mirrors a lot of superficial conversations that we have with each other.

Ionesco says: "A work of art is above all an adventure of the mind."

2. *The Wind-Up Bird Chronicle* is a huge novel by Japanese author Haruki Murakami. It follows the adventures of a young man whose cat disappears, and eventually his wife disappears too. Toru, the protagonist, is a seemingly simple guy; he cooks a lot of spaghetti and takes walks behind his apartment where there is an alley with a covered-over dried up well. During the course of the novel he keeps on looking at the well and thinking about exploring it. Filled with strange characters and traumatic memories of WW2, *The Wind-Up Bird Chronicle* may be my favorite MR novel and is one of my favorite novels period. It's an incredibly slow-paced book, but it is always extremely interesting because of how intently the hero, Toru, observes and interacts with the world. The book appeared in the mid 1990s.

I loved how slowly this story unfolds, and how the hero didn't do much – just like most of us. He sort of bumbles along and then eventually – very gradually –

discovers the person he can be. I also loved how every person he met had a wonderful story to tell – something that I wish would happen to me. This book helps me believe that even a regular person can do something brave and difficult, and can thereby make the world a bit more beautiful.

Murakami says: "In Japan they refer to the realistic style. They like answers and conclusions, but my stories have none. I want to leave them wide open to every possibility. I think my readers understand that openness."

3. *Cosmicomics* is a short story collection by Italian author Italo Calvino. These more or less linked stories tell about a family who lives through the entirety of global evolution. One of the early stories tells how uncomfortable the seating is for Grandmother before the Big Bang, and how happy she is when she finds a little pillow made of the first atoms. This collection came out in 1965.

I am terrible at science but I find dinosaurs and physics fascinating, so I loved how this collection plays with the imagery of scientific concepts (the Big Bang, dinosaur extinction), and uses those images to make up "impossible" stories.

Calvino says: "When I'm writing a book, I prefer not to speak about it, because only when the book is finished can I try to understand what I've really done. . ."

4. *The Famished Road*, a novel by Nigerian author Ben Okri, meshes spirit worlds with reality in an account of a spirit boy observing and interacting with his family, one member of whom wants to be a boxer. The book is written in English and appeared in 1991. It won the prestigious Booker Prize.

I loved the use of spirits and live people and the mixture of mythological and real worlds inhabiting the same space.

Okri says: "Our time here is magic! It's the only space you have to realize whatever it is that is beautiful, whatever is true, whatever is great, whatever is potential, whatever is rare, whatever is unique. It's the only space."

5. *Sexing the Cherry* is a novel by British author Jeanette Winterson. This novel veers back and forth between the present and 17th Century England and involves several different narrators as well as stories within stories about an enormous Dog Woman and her adopted quasi-son, Jordan. The novel was written in 1989. This book is so interesting because you don't always know what time period you're in but you are so

grounded in the reality of the moment, you don't care.

I loved the voice of the Dog-Woman and I loved the magical stories planted inside of the narrative. This novel really showed me that – to quote Aimee Bender – "as readers, we'll buy just about anything, as long as we are grounded in the world."

Winterson says: "I like to look at how people work together when they are put into stressful situations, when life stops being cozy."

6. Bonus Book! I'm including a book by our teacher, because it has exerted such a big influence on me. Aimee Bender's first collection of short stories, *The Girl in the Flammable Skirt* was published in the late 1990s. Written in straightforward, at times colloquial English, Bender's stories fool us into thinking they are simple stories, but they are anything but. These are fairy tales gone haywire, as a middle-aged mother of two gives birth to her dead mother, an erotically-minded librarian attempts to fix the fresco on the ceiling of the library where she works with the help of several male admirers, and a high-school romance blossoms between a mermaid and an imp, who are both trying to hide their magical identities. What constitutes a magic ability? Bender asks continually through these stories, and is being powerful a gift or a curse?

Who decides? What matters most, seems to be emotional connection and love – hard states of mind to achieve, especially when you are "different."

I loved the brave, strange female heroes of Bender's short story collection -- women and girls who dare to want and seek out dangerous people and dangerous situations in order to affirm who they really are, whether they are sexy librarians, or girls with a hand that is perpetually on fire.

Bender says: "Writing can be a frightening, distressing business, and whatever kind of structure or buffer is available can help a lot. For almost 17 years now, I've been faithful to a two-hours-a-day routine, every morning, five or six days a week. I get up, sit down, check e-mail briefly, turn off my e-mail and Internet, look at the time on the computer, write the two-hour marker on a little pad of paper on my desk, and begin."

Try this Little Writing Exercise

Now I want you to try something.

Look back at the book descriptions you just read and pick five words that struck you while you were reading.

For example:

Spaghetti
Dog
Famished
Fire chief
Rare

Now, very quickly write for 2-5 minutes using the words you've chosen. Try to make up a little story using all the words. Don't think too hard, just start writing and see where the words take you. (Note: if you'd like to know more about the process known as "free writing," turn to the end of this book for an explanation and some exercises)

Here's what I came up with.

```
What's for dinner?

    "The spaghetti is dog shaped," I
tell my husband.
```

"What kind of dog?" he asks and I say "a dachshund," and he says "won't that take too long to cook?"

I say "well what about spaghetti in the shape of a boxer? That will take even longer!"

"Wait a minute," he says, "that's not spaghetti, that's a noodle like macaroni!"

I shrug my shoulders. "I don't want to cook anyway." I stop filling the pot with water although I'm famished, because I haven't eaten in at least 100 years.

"Let's eat something different," he says, rustling his copy of *The Economist*. "How about reindeer burgers very rare?"

"No," I say. "No. I'm not hungry after all."

"But you have to eat!" he says. "As a fire chief you have to keep up your strength. You're the first female fire chief in our city, and what will they say if you collapse over the spaghetti controversy?"

"I don't know," I say. I open the refrigerator and look at all those pastas, barking and panting and

```
lifting their paws. Waiting to get
out.
```

This is just one example of one possible way to start a small, MR story. This is a first draft of something. I may do more with it. We'll see.

Put your little story aside, and let it look out the window or watch television.

I hope you had fun doing this exercise.

If you did, then you'll "get" why so many of us love Magical Realism. In the world of MR, we can encounter weird and fascinating authors, and then we can let our minds run wild, and use our own mundane world and problems (what's for dinner? What's in the refrigerator?) to generate stories that invoke and play with the impossible.

1. What IS Magical Realism?

When you join the world of Magical Realism, you meet and hang out with a fantastic group of writers from all over the world like:

Kathleen Alcalá (USA)
André Alexis (Canada)
Ryka Aoki (USA)
Aimee Bender (USA)
Roberto Bolaño (Chile)
Mikhail Bulgakov (Russia)
Italo Calvino (Italy)
Franz Kafka (Hungary)
Alain Mabanckou (Congo, France)
Yo Man (China)
Gabriel García Márquez (Columbia)
Toni Morrison (USA)
Haruki Murakami (Japan)
Ben Okri (Nigeria)
Patrick Süskind (Germany)
Jeanette Winterson (UK)

There are many online and real time discussions and disputes about what Magical Realism is and is not. I'm not sure that Toni Morrison would agree that *Beloved* is an example of MR, and Roberto Bolaño actually argued that he did NOT write Magical Realism and would yell if he saw himself on this list. There are active Facebook groups you can join where the qualities and characteristics of MR are fiercely debated, and there are other heated discussions going on online. As you explore the world of Magical Realism you can talk and argue with others too. This is an open and exciting international conversation.

But, there are two crucial definitions that most people agree on:

• Magical Realism is **not** a genre. As we just saw with my UCLA reading list, MR can "happen" in a play, a short story, or a novel. MR **is a mode or way of writing**, rather than a strict type, although it tends to tell some kind of story or "narrative" even if it's one where nothing happens.

• Magical Realism **does** something very specific: All MR juxtaposes the mundane and everyday with one or more unreal or impossible elements, and intensifies that juxtaposition during the course of the story or novel or play.

This means that, unlike fantasy novels such as the Harry Potter series, the Narnia books, or Neil Gaiman's *Neverwhere*, a magical domain or reality does not dominate the narrative. Rather, magical elements intervene on the everyday world OR the two (or more) realms co-exist in the same space in such a way that the reader isn't sure which one is the "real" one.

Remember, Magical Realism is all about the juxtaposition between the magical/unreal/impossible and the mundane everyday world.

2. How does Magical Realism work?

It's tempting to think of a literary mode as a list of static qualities that simply get put into a box labeled "Magical Realism." But for us writers, a more useful image of Magical Realism is that of a recipe. We have a list of ingredients, sure. But the best way for us to understand a mode of writing is to get a sense for how it combines the ingredients and cooks up the recipe.

Let's take a look at Gabriel García Márquez's short short story "The Handsomest Drowned Man in the World." You can borrow this story from a collection at your local library or access it in English at a number of websites or you can purchase a copy of Márquez's short stories. And if you can read it in Spanish -- all the better!

Márquez's story works according to one very simple idea. Local children find a dead body that has washed up on the beach. The corpse gets bigger and bigger as more and more people see and handle it. It increases in size, weight, and beauty, until it changes the lives of the villagers and of everyone who comes into contact with it.

Let's use Márquez's story to help us write.

Writing exercise
A. With a friend, family member, or on your own, list 10 things that you would normally find at the beach.

1.
2.

3.

4.

5.

6.

7.

8.

9.

10.

B. Pick one of these things, or have a friend or family pick one for you.

C. Now think about a place that is as far away from the beach as possible, both geographically and psychologically. Here are some suggestions:

1. A MacDonald's
2. A FedEx/Kinko's or other photocopying store
3. A circulation desk at the library
4. A children's school playground
5. A doctor's office waiting room
6. IRS headquarters
7. A museum cloakroom

D. Let's write
- Now write 2-3 sentences about finding that beach-thing in that non-beach place.
- In the next couple of sentences make that thing get larger or change it in some physical way.
- Change the reactions of the people who have found it. 2-3 sentences.

- Change the thing again. 2-3 sentences.
- Bring in more people and make them have bigger/different reactions. 2-3 sentences.
- Change the thing one more time. 2-3 sentences.
- Bring in someone from very far away who sees/experiences the thing from their own point of view. What do they say? 2-3 sentences.

Congratulations! You just wrote the beginning of a magical realist story. You may even have a complete first draft or perhaps you have an idea for a longer story.

Don't like what you wrote? Try another combination. Or flip the exercise. Make a list of things you usually find in an office and put one of them on a mountaintop or in a forest. Now what happens?

E. If you look back at your story and compare it with Márquez's you will see that both stories work by:

1. Establishing the juxtaposition between the usual and the strange/impossible.

2. Continually growing the situation, making it literally and figuratively bigger and bigger, and then shifting the point of view at the very end.

Note: Many ancient stories work on the basis of a physical transformation. The Roman writer Ovid wrote a series of stories-in-verse called *The Metamorphoses*, which recount famous transformations from Greco-Roman mythology.

Physical transformation is a crucial element of many fairy tales including "The Frog Prince," "The Twelve Brothers," the 18th Century fairy tale "Beauty and the Beast," and the 19th Century fairy tale "The Little Mermaid."

These sorts of transformations are used *a lot* in Magical Realism.

Here are a few examples:
- Both Kafka's *The Metamorphosis* and Aimee Bender's "The Rememberer" use physical transformation as the jumping off point for the story.
- Kafka's protagonist Gregor Samsa wakes up to find himself transformed into a giant cockroach in his famous story.
- "The Rememberer" operates on a premise, which is the opposite of the Márquez story. The protagonist's boyfriend de-evolves into a monkey, a turtle, and lizard and onward. So, he gets smaller and smaller instead of bigger as the story progresses.
- Like Kafka, Robert Olen Butler has his protagonist turn into an animal in his short story "Jealous Husband Returns in Form of a Parrot."

Dramatic physical change to a main character is a fantastic way to make a story feel emotionally intense and exciting. It's also a great way to introduce humor into the picture. There is something funny about Gregor the salesman turning into a giant bug, and there is something decidedly ludicrous in the fact that Butler's jealous husband returns – not as a scary monster – but as a bird who can only repeat over and over again the words that have been said to it by the humans.

3. Plot and Character: Understanding and Using the Fairy Tale Model

We've seen that Magical Realism mixes the mundane with the impossible or supernatural, which it then intensifies in some way.

Now we'll talk about story structure.

If you look at Magical Realist fiction, you'll notice that underneath all the flying carpets, salesmen turning into insects and devolving boyfriends the actual story line is usually fairly straightforward and/or familiar. This is certainly the case with the "Handsomest Drowned Man in the World," which we looked at in the previous chapter.

Many writers who work with Magical Realism look to the folk or fairy tale as an influence. Aimee Bender actually teaches courses on fairy tales, and Ryka Aoki very self-consciously uses Hawaiian folklore as an inspiration in her amazing novel *He Mele A Hilo*.

The Russian folklorist Vladimir Propp argued that fairy and folk tales could be broken down into tiny segments, the he called "narratemes." In his book, *The Morphology of a Russian Folktale,* Propp observes four different "spheres of action" in the fairy tale and as many as 31 narratemes operating within a given story.

Not all stories have all 31 elements, but it's almost impossible for a story not to have any.

Here is the full list of Vladimir Propp's narratemes, courtesy of the lovely people over at changing minds.org.

1st Sphere: Introduction

Steps 1 to 7 introduces the situation and most of the main characters, setting the scene for subsequent adventure.

- 1. Absentation: Someone goes missing
- 2. Interdiction: Hero is warned
- 3. Violation of interdiction
- 4. Reconnaissance: Villain seeks something
- 5. Delivery: The villain gains information
- 6. Trickery: Villain attempts to deceive victim
- 7. Complicity: Unwitting helping of the enemy

2nd Sphere: The Body of the story

The main story starts here and extends to the departure of the hero on the main quest.

- 8. Villainy and lack: The need is identified
- 9. Mediation: Hero discovers the lack
- 10. Counteraction: Hero chooses positive action
- 11. Departure: Hero leave on mission

3rd Sphere: The Donor Sequence

In the third sphere, the hero goes in search of a method by which the solution may be reached, gaining the magical agent from the Donor. Note that this in itself may be a complete story.

- 12. Testing: Hero is challenged to prove heroic qualities
- 13. Reaction: Hero responds to test
- 14. Acquisition: Hero gains magical item
- 15. Guidance: Hero reaches destination

- 16. Struggle: Hero and villain do battle
- 17. Branding: Hero is branded
- 18. Victory: Villain is defeated
- 19. Resolution: Initial misfortune or lack is resolved

4th Sphere: The Hero's return

In the final (and often optional) phase of the storyline, the hero returns home, hopefully uneventfully and to a hero's welcome, although this may not always be the case.

- 20. Return: Hero sets out for home
- 21. Pursuit: Hero is chased
- 22. Rescue: pursuit ends
- 23. Arrival: Hero arrives unrecognized
- 24. Claim: False hero makes unfounded claims
- 25. Task: Difficult task proposed to the hero
- 26. Solution: Task is resolved
- 27. Recognition: Hero is recognised
- 28. Exposure: False hero is exposed
- 29. Transfiguration: Hero is given a new appearance
- 30. Punishment: Villain is punished
- 31. Wedding: Hero marries and ascends the throne

Yikes! That's a lot of narratemes!

Does this system even work? You are wondering.

Let's take a look at Erin Martinsen's plot analysis of the Disney movie *Cinderella*, using Propp's terms:

1 – **Absentation.** The father dies after remarrying the stepmother, leaving Cinderella with only stepfamily.

2 – **Interdiction.** Cinderella is turned from a family member into a worker.

6 – **Trickery.** The stepmother tells Cinderella she may be able to attend the ball, though she doesn't plan to ever allow that to happen.

7 – **Complicity.** Cinderella believes she may be allowed to attend the ball if she completes her chores.

12 – **First Donor Function.** Cinderella is punished by the stepmother and banned from the ball.

13 – **Hero reacts to actions of Donor.** In the 1950 film, the mice helpers offer Cinderella advice before the fairy godmother appears.

14 – **Receipt of Agent.** Fairy godmother appears and dresses Cinderella.

15 – **Guidance.** The fairy godmother guides Cinderella to the ball.

21 – **Hero is pursued.** The prince searches for Cinderella.

24 – **Unfounded claims.** The stepmother tries to pass off her daughters as the owners of the slipper.

25 – **Difficult task presented to Hero.** Cinderella has to make the prince recognize her.

26 – **Solution.** Cinderella is freed from her lockup and is able to try on the slipper.

27 – **Hero is recognized.** The slipper fits Cinderella.

28 – **Exposure.** Stepmother is exposed as a villain.

30 – **Villain is punished.** Different versions have variations on how the stepmother is punished.

31 – Cinderella marries the prince, and lives **happily ever after.**

Wow! It works!

These would be the kinds of plot elements, your own magical realist story might talk to or riff on. Your story might not be quite this complicated, but it would certainly contain at least some of these elements.

Now, let's try to write a fairy tale using Propp's ideas!

Writing Exercise --

A. List 7 "absentations." Don't overthink it. Just list whatever comes to mind. I give you three examples just to get you started.

1. Mother goes away on Mediterranean cruise for 10 weeks but doesn't come back.

2. Boyfriend drops out of school and refuses to come out of his apartment.

3. Therapist goes on alcoholic bender and is hospitalized.

4.

5.

6.

7.

8.

9.

10.

B. Now look at your list. Circle the 2 or 3 absentations that seem interesting to you.

C. Choose one and write a few sentences of the beginning of a story about this absentation.

D. Now write a few sentences answering each of the following questions. Feel free to introduce a magical power, element, or object at any point in the story, but don't use more than 5 or so of such elements.

- Tell us who is the person who has been affected by this change? (That's your protagonist)
- What downturn in their lives has happened?
- Who or what now tries to hurt them? How?

- How does that hurt succeed?
- How is the protagonist changed by what has happened?
- What does the protagonist do in response to that hurt?
- Who helps the protagonist?
- What do they receive from other sources?
- How does the protagonist change?
- Do they win or lose or do they leave the world of the battle altogether?

You've just written a draft of a fairy tale structured story!

You can do this exercise any time you like. Pick another absentation from your list or start again. You can also ask a friend or relative to make a list of absentations. Sometimes it's great to get an assignment from another person, because they think in a completely different way and care about different things than you do.

Here's my first attempt at a story following these instructions:

Mom said she was going on a Mediterranean cruise. She always wanted to go on one, but her work at the peanut shelling plant always kept her from doing the things she really wanted. Well, one day, she announced that she was DONE shelling peanuts, and she was going to Istanbul and Rome and Barcelona like she always wanted.

The trouble was she left... and she hasn't come back.

Terry gets these postcards from her. *Having a great time in Monaco,* said one. *Won at slots and met a prince.*

Now there's no one to take care of the house. I can't cook and neither can Terry, and we've just finished college, and we don't have any money. And the vacuum cleaner's broken. And we are out of Swiffers.

The landlord says it's pay up or get out.

I go to Walmart to apply for the Greeting job.

The Walmart supervisor says I have to smile bigger than that. He gives me a job scrubbing floors.

This is a crap place to work, says the lady who scrubs the floors next to me. I think you should go smile in some better place. I say I want to but how?

I scrub and I scrub. The supervisor says I need to work longer hours but my pay can't go up because I'm really just an intern. My hands become stained by the cleanser, which is blue like the Mediterranean.

That's a pretty color blue says the lady in the next aisle. Your hands are too pretty to be working here. You need a better place.

One night I'm at home and a lawyer on the TV says something about illegal work practices. I take his number. I go to his office. He's super handsome. He says your hands are like the ocean. So beautiful. I smile. I kiss him because I'm lonely, and he's so handsome and so nice. He gives me some free advice.

I go back to work and videotape my work day.

I sue the supervisor.

I get enough money to pay the rent, and I realize I really like cleaning. So I become a professional house cleaner. It's fun making things bright.

And I don't have to smile unless I want to.

The name of my company: Istanbul
Blue. The lawyer helps me set it up.
Bob. He's so sweet.

I hire my neighbor from next
aisle over at Walmart. Terry does the
bookkeeping. He's great at computers.

I send my mom a postcard....
Well, I write it and drop it in the
ocean near my house.

I miss you Mom, I write.

*But me and Terry -- we're just
fine.*

There are some things I will change about this
story, but I've got the absentation, interdiction, villain,
helpers, and donors. I've even got two princes -- the one
the mother gets, and the lawyer! It's a bit light on
magic, but that's ok. I can add more magic into it in the
second draft.

==

Another way into this story is through the
character types.

Here is Erin Martinsen's list of characters from
Cinderella. Once again, she is borrowing Vladimir
Propp's typology of characters.

The hero: Cinderella

The villain(s): The evil stepmother

The magical helper: The fairy godmother

The donors: the mice... lesser helpers or gift givers

The father: the one who dies (C's dad), and the one who sends the Prince on his mission to get married (his father)

False hero(es): the stepsisters

[**The dispatcher** -- person who sends the hero out on the quest -- is missing in this story, but is a character that Propp thinks is important to a folk or fairy tale]

Let's work with these!

Writing Exercise:

A. List 8 chores you have to do or errands you need to run at your business/school or around town.

Here are a couple of examples.

1. Get cash at the cash machine.
2. Help at the Girl Scout cookie sales table.
3.
4.
5.
6.
7.
8.
9.
10.

B. Circle 1 or 2 of these errands/chores that strike you in some way.

C. Now write a scene or story based on the errand/chore you've chosen that features at least these 3 characters:
    magical helper
    villain
    Hero

D. (Note on plot) Have the hero get tricked or fail in some way at least once.

These exercises can help you understand a bit how you best work as a writer. Some writers feel comfortable with a set of plot assignments (I'm one of those people). Others do better working with characters. Hopefully both of these exercises can be the beginnings of some stories that you can further develop and then sound out for publication.

My idea: the princess has to go to the cash machine, because the king has run out of checks and it will take time for the new checks to arrive.

4. Style, Part 1: Languaging Magically

We just saw that although the plot of a magical realist story or novel can be simple, the juxtaposition of elements can make the story feel rich and complicated.

Another way to "magically realize" your story is through language. Once again, juxtaposition is a key idea.

There are two basic ways to make your story have a magical realist feel:

1. Magic-ize the everyday, by using language that stresses the fairy tale, unreal, and/or point to an alternate reality which is completely inappropriate to the matter at hand.

2. Use realistic language to make the magical seem mundane.

Award winning author Bruce Holland Rogers puts it clearly: "magical realist writers write the ordinary as miraculous and the miraculous as ordinary."

Let's try playing with magical/extraordinary language.

Exercise 1.

A. Make a detailed list of the things you did this morning to get ready for work/school. For example:

1. Walked into the bathroom.

2. Peed and brushed teeth.

3. Put on bathrobe.

4. Walked into kitchen and poured coffee.

5. Walked outside with coffee and sat and looked at the backyard.

6. Answered the phone.

7. Sat down at computer.

8. Argued with husband about how clean the house was.

B. Now write a short paragraph about your morning, where you describe everything you did in terms of being a

1. Fairy tale hero/villain/helper

2. Astronaut

3. A robotics expert

4. A cowboy or cowgirl

5. Your choice!

To do this exercise, you'll want to consult some online sources that list these sorts of words. See how many words from the list you can cram into your paragraph. The appendix on page 95 has some lingo lists, but feel free to find your own lists:

Here's what two of my opening sentences looked like:

```
1. Once upon a time, Princess
Stephanie awakened from an enchanted
```

```
slumber to feel a tingling in her
bladder.
    2. At T-minus 30 minutes to
blastoff, Captain Hammer expelled
waste in 30.4 seconds and donned suit
model Alpha B requisite for the
upcoming mission.
```

The point of this exercise is to experience how highly specialized language can make even the most mundane story -- i.e. getting up in the morning and going to the bathroom -- pop with excitement and humor.

C. You can develop this story further, remembering to make the juxtaposition bigger and bigger as you go along.

Exercise 2. Technical and specialized language.

A. Go to your local library or go online and look for dictionaries, technical encyclopedias or any resource that lists and defines words. These could be books on dentistry or books on beer-making.

B. Take a look at 3-5 books, picking at random. For each of these books, make your own list of 5-10 words that strike you.

For example, I pulled these from an exterminator website:

Action Thresholds --An action threshold is the point at which an IPM technician takes action to reduce a pest's numbers. Below the designated pest level, control action isn't normally taken.

Application --Applying a product to manage pests.

Bait stations --Bait stations are containers used to house bait for pests such as ants, cockroaches or rodents. Stations vary in appearance depending on type and model. Typically placed near harborage areas, a bait station should allow for easy monitoring of bait levels, sometimes by using clear view ports.

Botulism --A form of food poisoning generally caused by the ingestion of a toxin stemming from improper storage of food or beverages.

Commensal --Rodents are commensal in nature, which means to "share one's table." These rodents are able to thrive in human environments. The main three commensal rodents are Norway rats, roof rats, and house mice.

C.   Now use the words from this lexicon to talk about something that is the opposite of calling the exterminator, like: having sex, serving dinner at a fancy restaurant, praying in a church, mosque, temple or other secret place, or telling a small child a fairy tale at night.

Note: This use of what the Russian Formalists called "defamiliarization" is a technique used by writers like George Saunders as well as by Booker prize-winning writer Kazuo Ishiguro. Both of them like to disguise the horror of a situation by using strange vocabulary for it. In the "Semplica Girls Diary," Saunders uses an acronym to partially conceal the characters' ghastly practice of hanging immigrant girls in residential gardens as lawn ornaments. In *Never Let Me Go*, Ishiguro has the clone protagonist talk about being killed off in their capacity as organ donors as "completing."

This is a technique to think about if you like to write very dark stories or have a macabre imagination.

In our next chapter we will talk about style and how we can mesh new and different words with a new and different point of view.

5. Style, Part 2: Who's Talking? A Note on Point of View

My Norwegian relatives in the Ballard neighborhood of Seattle had a somewhat uncertain relationship to the English language (their first language was Norwegian, of course), and they were busy people -- farming, plumbing, hairdressing, and baking.

So when they answered a ringing telephone, they liked to get right to the point:

"Who's talking?" was their opening greeting.

Who's talking matters in any kind of story. One of the most fun elements of Magical Realism is that ANYONE (or any<u>thing</u>) can tell the story. And this gives you a tremendous amount of freedom.

In our last chapter, we talked a little about the kinds of words we can use to tell a magical realist story.

Now let's talk about point of view.

Languaging is directly connected to the person telling the story, so when we change the point of view from which the story is told, we have the opportunity to do some fun things with words.

Classic fairy tales are all written in third person ("once upon a time there was a .... And he or she did this and this") and are told from a more or less "objective" point of view.

What would happen if you took your favorite fairy tale and told it in the first person, from a vantage point other than the hero's?

That's what exactly what I do with my story "Do Not Mess around with the Virgin Mary" -- which is a reboot of a Grimm Brothers story called "Mary's Child."

Let's take a look.

Do Not Mess around with the Virgin Mary

People, all I can say is:
Do NOT mess around with the Virgin Mary.

I'm nice; as you may know, I'm the mother of the J-man, who is God after all. But I just have to tell you - do NOT PISS ME OFF. I know when you are lying. I know when you are sleeping etc. Sort of like Santa Claus, but slimmer with a nice blue veil, and a classy demeanor. In other words I know what you are doing and when you're doing it, and I know what you're doing, even when I'm not home. I'm away a lot because, I HAVE A LOT TO DO.

Like that girl I rescued from Ojai. Her parents were these down and out hippies. They'd been growing weed, but that business failed because they smoked all their product, and they were basically starving, and their little girl was crying in the preschool parking lot, so I came down to their beat up Volkswagen bus and said "I shall care for the child," and up we went to Heaven.

In case you didn't know, Heaven is a fabulous property that looks just like Big Sur. There are gorgeous trees, and an amazing view of the ocean and seals that come and play on the beach, and of course scrumptious organic cocktails, and humus, and a lovely gift shop and all kinds of places to stay: cabins, and designer tents, and luxury tree houses.

Because -- duh - your father's house has many mansions.

Yes, it's THAT house we're talking about, with gardens and endless vistas and excellent weather.

So, I give the little girl the keys to the entire complex, and tell her "Sweetie, you should enjoy! Go wherever you want, play in every playroom, enjoy the spa, go horseback riding, but stay out of the 13th tree house, which is used for storage."

So, I leave because I have visitations to make and saints to talk to and jugglers to see juggle at my altars, and -- what can I tell you? -- I'm a popular lady.

But, what do you think happens? That kid goes into every room and plays with the Apostle in each one. I hear that James plays videogames, and Simon plays ping-pong, and Peter tells the best bedtime stories – which figures. But the little girl -- let's call her Britte -- she wants that 13th room: the tree house. The little angels say no, and the big angels say no, and the flowers say no and the birds say no, but she goes in and sees the Holy Ghost roasting marshmallows over a big camp fire, and she puts her hand out to take one, and her finger turns gold.

I come back and – what's a mother to do? -- I throw her out. She goes and lives in the wilderness out by Joshua Tree, and then she meets some guy (which is nice and of which I approve) but when I say to her "Britte, I need you to take responsibility for this Holy Ghost and some mores situation," she has the gall to deny it.

"No Virgin Mary, I did not go into the 13th room," she pipes up in this very annoying SoCal voice, and she keeps on denying, which is -- let's face it -- very inadequate and immature.

Well, she marries the guy who runs some software empire, and she has a kid.

"Young lady," I intone in the Cedars Sinai Maternity Ward. "Didn't you go into that 13th room?" She says no, so I take the baby.

But she doesn't listen. Why don't they EVER listen?

She has 2 more kids and I take THEM away too.

Oh, and I don't let her speak, because I'm STRICT LIKE THAT.

What does she do? Nothing. She keeps on denying until the town is about to burn her as a witch at the Palm Desert mall. The citizens say she's much too quiet to be a good person, and what did she DO with those three kids?

So they get ready to burn her at the stake. Yes, I know that's an overreaction. But people don't like it when you go all quiet and seem to have apparently devoured your own progeny.

That's when Britte says "Oh gosh, I'm sorry I opened the 13th door!" just as the flames are about to melt some of that juvederm she had put in her lips.

And I say, "That's all you had to do, <u>bubbe</u>." I give her the kids back, and her voice, and I do a little liposuction while I'm at it. Because I want that she should look nice for her husband after all this <u>tsuris</u>.

So the moral is: seriously, don't mess around with the Virgin Mary, or you'll have to live in the wilderness and almost get burned alive at a mall and--I'm just saying – it's NOT WORTH IT.

A couple of things are happening here.
- I choose to tell the story from the point of view of a character who is not the hero (that person is ostensibly the young girl whom Mary adopts).
- I take literally the idea that Jesus was Jewish and make the Virgin Mary a modern-day, controlling Jewish mother, complete with a Yiddish

vocabulary and an over-the-top attitude. (I happen to be a Jewish writer so I feel very at home writing in this way.) As a result the languaging of the narrator is completely at odds with the subject matter -- making the story (hopefully) comical. In other words, I use mundane language to tell a magical story.

A. Let's try the following exercises. Remember to use the first person. "I did this. I saw that."

1. Tell the beginning of "Little Red Riding Hood" from the Wolf's point of view. How does a wolf talk anyway? (Interesting question) It would depend on the wolf.

Suggestion: Think about how the following "wolves" might talk.

- A predatory privileged fraternity boy at college. Which college? Big or small?
- A male supervisor at Walmart. What department does he run? How old is he? Is he married?

2. Tell the beginning of "Hansel and Gretel" from Gretel's point of view.

Suggestion: Think about how the following "Gretel's" might express themselves and get as specific as possible about who they are.

- Is Gretel a high-school student? Is she a person of faith? Which faith?

- Is she a middle-grade student with a learning difference? What town/region is she from? That will change how she talks.

3. Tell the beginning of "The Frog Prince" story from the frog's point of view.

4. Tell the beginning of the story of "Sleeping Beauty" from the bad fairy's point of view.

5. Tell the beginning of the story of "Cinderella" from one of the evil sisters' points of view.

B. Try writing the first few paragraphs of any or all of the above stories. Ask yourself some questions about your point of view characters. Here are a few suggestions:

- What kinds of aspects of life would a human/frog think about?
- What's the bad fairy's backstory? Why does she get so mad so easily? How old is she and what have her relationships been like?
- Same goes for the evil sisters. What are their hobbies? What are their insecurities? What's their favorite food? Which one of them does the mother like better?

C. If the writing is going well, finish the story! Chances are one of these will spark something interesting. If not, no worries, you're just practicing.

A-C variation 1. You can also re-tell the fairytale from a side-character's point of view. Try these:

1. What happens to "Little Red Riding Hood" if you tell it from the woodsman's point of view or the mother's?
2. What about if "The Frog Prince" is told from the king's point of view? Or the man-servant to the prince, who appears in some versions of the story? Or perhaps a real frog could befriend the Frog Prince and comment on the action!
3. Speaking of animals, how might those little birds tell the story of "Cinderella?" (Note: the original story is MUCH more violent than the Disney version so be sure to check it out, because the birds have a big part in it!).

A-C variation 2. An object can tell the story too! Most fairy tales have important objects in them, and these can tell the story of what they see/experience. For example:

1. Tell the story of "Little Red Riding Hood" from the points of view of the basket, the path, the actual house that belongs to Grandmother, or even the woodsman's axe. And what about that famous cape of hers? Doesn't that cape have a story to tell?

2. Tell the story of "The Frog Prince" from the point of view of the bouncing ball, the dinnerware, the pond or the wall.

3. Tell the story of "Sleeping Beauty" from the point of view of the castle, the spindle, or the hedge.

6. Style, Part 3: Go Big -- Multiple Points of View AND Time

If you want to go really crazy as a writer -- and after all, MR is all about pushing the envelope -- you can tell your story using multiple points of view. A famous novel by Juan Rulfo does just this. Rulfo's short but powerful novel *Pedro Páramo* takes the reader through the strange adventure of a young man searching for his father in a deserted town. But as soon as the hero Juan Preciado arrives, other people (often not immediately identified) interrupt and tell their stories about the town and Juan's father too. They all speak in first person!

The story goes back and forth in time without warning as well. At one point in the novel, near the end of the book we are suddenly faced with the point of view of Pedro Páramo as a small boy, although we've been told repeatedly that he died a long time ago.

In an even wilder iteration of these ideas, Sesshu Foster's novel *Atomik Aztex* veers between two very different realities. One story line is narrated from the point of view of a worker at a sausage killing floor in East LA. The narrator is a modern day Aztec warrior who is fighting World War II in an alternate reality where Aztec culture has triumphed over the West but not yet over Hitler. We never learn which reality is the "true" one.

Let's play with these ideas.

A. Point of view --

1. Look back at the exercises that you've done with in chapter 5, and select the fairy tale that you find the most fun to retell.

2. Now, try interspersing 2-3 points of view in it. Keep them all in the first person. You can use what you've already written for these items, or write something new. Or you can do both!

Here are a few suggestions for a mash-up of points of view:

- How might the woodsman's axe, Little Red Riding Hood's cape (or hood, or hat), and the grandmother's house take turns telling the story of their lives and what happened with LRR?
- For "Cinderella", the birds (using first person plural, "we"), one or both of the evil stepsisters, ("I" or "We") and the shoe(s) that only Cinderella can fit on her feet (again "I" or "we").
- "Sleeping Beauty," told from the points of view of all 13 fairies. Or from the points of view of the servants and the spindle.

B. Hey! What about time?

Try writing 1 or more points of view that narrate events at different moments in or outside the timeline of the story. Here are some suggestions to play with:

- What is Little Red Riding Hood's mother doing before she gets married? Does she get married at all? What was her relationship with her mother (the grandmother) like? Or, is the grandmother her mother-in-law?

- What happens to the family after this Wolf-eating-Grandma incident? How are their lives changed?

- What's the history of the town where this fairy tale happens? Might there be a librarian or town archivist who has recorded it? What other animal-related crimes or crimes against elders have happened in the town already? Or have they had very different sorts of issues in their community? Like what?

- What political issues is the town dealing with at the same time as the tale unfolds? Is the woodsman a union member? What kind of job does the mother have, or does she have one? What does the American Association of Retired Persons think about Grandma being stuck in that cabin by herself in the woods? What lumber company wants to move in and take over and clear-cut the forest?

C. Things to think about:

- Working with multiple points of view as well as points of time are offer us great ways to explore what parts of a story feel alive and exciting as well as complex.

- What may happen is that one or two viewpoints will "pop" much more than the others. That's fine.
- Or, it may happen that all the points of view feel terrific. If so, that's great. Your resulting story will probably feel a bit dream-like, since the reality that your story has created is made up of many different views of what that reality is. Just like *Pedro Páramo* and *Atomik Aztex* where we aren't entirely sure who is alive and who is dead or where we even are in history, and we aren't sure what is real and what is imagined. *

This is precisely one of the questions that Magical Realism is asking--what is real, and who decides?

At the end of his story "Macario," B. Traven leaves it to us to decide whether Macario's magical encounter with the Bone Man was a dream or not and wonder what it was that actually killed him. The author accomplishes this feat, by shifting the point of view at the very end of the story, from Macario to his wife.

Here's what Foster's Aztec Zenzontli has to say about the topic of the real:

Cuz in no way does that fit our aesthetic conception of how the universe is supposed to run. It's just plain ugly. To think that they want to foist that vision of Reality on the rest of us. That's the insult. Barbarik, cheap aesthetik based on flimsy Mechanistik notions of the omniverse as a Swiss watch set to ticking by some sort of Trinity. The Spanish believed they had superior firepower with their gunpowder, blunderbusses, crossbows with metal darts, steel body armor, Arabian horses, galleons built in Cadiz. All that wuz true. But we Aztex had our ways and means. We have access to the meanest nastiest psycho Gods through voodoo, jump blues human sacrifice, proletarian vanguard parties, Angry Coffeehouse Poetry, fantasy life intensified thru masturbation & comic books, plus all out armies, Flower Warriors, Jaguar Legions, Eagle Elite Units, Jiu Jitsu and of course the secret weapon. (*Atomik Aztex*)

D. Recap – cooking up a fairy tale reboot

Here once again are the 6 basic ingredients for your fairy tale reboot. You can always mess with the story later. But for your first draft, do follow these guidelines.

1. Choose a classic fairy tale that you like. It could be "Hansel and Gretel," or "Cinderella," or you can look up a lesser-known fairy tale from a collection like the Grimm Brothers.

2. Read your fairy tale carefully. If it helps, you can make notes of the most important things that happen. If there are numbers involved (3 wishes, 12 fairies) you might want to write those down.

3. Write your own version of the story, using first person and speaking in a vernacular or slang that this person would talk in. Note: here's your opportunity to use your own language(s) and ethnicity/ies when writing your new version of the story. Think about who's talking. The narrator can be the original hero, the villain, or the magical helper, or even a secondary character or object.

4. Consider telling telling the story from the point(s) of view of characters who are not the hero.

5. Consider playing with time, and having your point of view characters relate events that happen, before, during, or after the main storyline.

6. STAY TRUE TO THE PLOT (at least in your first draft).

----

*Compare this magical realist uncertainty of these stories to Kurt Vonnegut's time warp novel *Slaughterhouse Five*. In his book, we know exactly what is happening and why, because the author gives Billy Pilgrim's time-travel a scientific explanation.

7. Other Story Reboots to Try

The traditional story reboot is a wonderful way to stretch your story-telling muscles and interact creatively with material that you love and/or that challenges you. We have focused on the classic fairy tale as a model, but there are many others to learn about and use. Ben Okri uses Nigerian folklore as the basis for *The Famished Road* while Ryka Aoki looks to Hawaiian gods and goddesses for material in her magical realist novel about hula dancing, *He Mele a Hilo*. Leslie Marmon Silko meshes different strands of Pueblo myth and belief (she is 1/4 Laguna Pueblo) in her powerful novel about a mixed race WW2 vet, *Ceremony*.

A. Working with the ancestors prompt: What folkloric and/or mythology traditions can you look to personally for inspiration? Where are your older family members from originally? Do some research online. Then make a list of plot points and characters that interest you.

Example: My ancestors are from Norway and Russia originally. I might do research online about the Norse gods and about Russian folklore and mine that material for stories and characters that I can play with. I look for the telling detail that can generate something.

My list might look something like this:

1. Odin sacrifices his eye so that he can learn the future of the world. Story idea: a very nearsighted

61

person gives up their eyeglasses so they can "see" something no-one else can see in a small town.

2. Baba Yaga in her house in the woods that spins around on chicken legs. Sometimes she has a mop or broom with her. Story idea: Baba Yaga becomes a professional housecleaner in big cosmopolitan city like Seattle.

Now try making up your own list of possible story ideas from folklore/mythology related to your ancestry. Again, look for the telling detail or the newly discovered aspect:

1.
2.
3.
4.
5.
6.
7.
8.
9.
10.

B. Working with the Greek Mythology and the Bible. Greek Mythology has been a source of inspiration for writers ever since the *Iliad*, and this subject matter has appealed to people of very different ethnic and religious backgrounds. Franz Kafka--a Jew in Prague (part of the Austro-Hungarian Empire)--wrote a strange and wonderful flash fiction piece about Poseidon, whom he has turned into an office accountant.

Poseidon is bored out of his mind with counting all the fish in the sea. More recently, Afro-Canadian writer André Alexis, stages a bar conversation in the present day between the Greek gods Apollo and Hermes, where they make a wager about dogs. This is the set up for his award-winning novel *Fifteen Dogs*. Likewise, the Bible is a wonderful source for storytelling. Nikos Kazantzakis' ambitious and controversial novel *The Last Temptation of Christ* portrays Jesus as a real person (and a truly Jewish person), who may or may not actually be the Messiah.

Do some research online or at the library and make a list of possible story ideas/ characters from Greek mythology and/or from the Bible or other sacred scripture. Note: for both of these, it's useful to look at lesser known ideas and characters. Alexis uses Hermes -- a less understood god -- in his pairing, and Kazantzakis focuses on the character and point of view of Judas (who in his retelling is a passionate political revolutionary).

Make a list of possible story ideas/characters here:

1.
2.
3.
4.
5.

6.

7.

8.

9.

10.

C. Look back at both your lists, and circle 2-5 ideas that excite you.

D. Pick one and write about it.

E. Things to keep in mind:

- Remember that Magical Realism is about **the juxtaposition** between the magical and the mundane. In his novel *The Master and Margarita*, Mikhail Bulgakov retells the Faust legend by situating it in the early Soviet Union and having the characters deal with the bureaucracy and party politics of that place and time.

- How can your character/situation conflict with the everyday world? How can that conflict grow?

- How can you use the original plot connected to your folkloric/mythical/biblical character/situation/idea in the action of your story? Bulgakov follows the plot points of the Faust story quite closely.

8. Magical Realism and Non-Happy Endings

So far we've been talking about Magical Realism and the fairy tale. Fairy tales always end happily.

But Magical Realist stories and novels do not necessarily end in this way. In fact, many MR stories are extremely sad.

A. Magical Realism and the Tragic

Aimee Bender's short story "The Rememberer" is a case in point. A woman tells the story of how her boyfriend devolves first into being a monkey, and then into a salamander. The narrator tries and tries to prevent the devolution of the man she loves, but in the end she does the following:

> I put him in the passenger seat of the car, and drive him to the beach. Walking down the sand, I nod at people on towels, laying their bodies out to the sun and wishing. At the water's edge, I stoop down and place the whole pan on the tip of a baby wave. It floats well, a cooking boat, for someone to find washed up on shore and to make cookies in, a lucky catch for a poor soul with all the ingredients but no container. Ben the salamander swims out. I wave to the water with both arms, big enough for him to see if he looks back.

This story, and other famous MR stories like Franz Kafka's "The Metamorphosis, and George Saunders' "Sea Oak" have endings that are so sad they gesture towards tragedy.

Again, it's helpful to use our recipe analogy when thinking about how tragedy works. Most of us have learned about something called "hubris" and the so-called "tragic fall." My teacher Eugene Falk argued for a different, more active way of understanding tragedy. Falk argued that tragedy happens when the hero/protagonist renounces something or someone. Renunciation is not the same as sacrifice, in his view. We renounce something or someone that we really deeply want. We give it up, in order to affirm something more important, a personal value that we hold dear. The tension between the love we have for the thing/person and the value that is crucial to our identity and sense of self is what makes tragedy feel tragic.

In Bender's story, the narrator renounces the boyfriend, whom she dearly loves. But she values her memory of him (of who he was) more than hanging on to the disappearing physical being that he is. She literally sets this being free, and in so doing retains her enormous love for him, her respect for him as a person, and her valuing of love as a transcendent ideal, that is more than either of them.

Something similarly grand happens to Kafka's Gregor Samsa, despite the fact that he has been transformed into an enormous cockroach. His love of music and his forgiveness of his family make him more human than the family who survives him. They are the monsters. He is not.

In an intriguing twist on the transformation trope, Heather Fowler's novel *Beautiful Ape Girl Baby* gives us an oversized female protagonist who has no idea that she is a monster, because she is carefully secluded and protected by her rich father, even when she escapes from the family compound and ostensibly embarks on a wild picaresque adventure. It is only in the final pages of the book, that Beautiful realizes that society regards her as an grotesque simian aberration, at the same time as she finally grasps the full extent to which her father has successfully determined and shaped almost every encounter she has had on her adventure. Rather than succumb to the opinions of others and the control of her father, Beautiful makes a tragic choice. She renounces life itself, affirming an almost Existentialist sense of freewill, as she literally throws herself off a cliff, and subsequently drowns herself in the ocean.

Writing Exercise – tragic transformations

1. Make a list of magical or impossible ways that a protagonist or someone that the protagonist loves could be "transformed."

a. Protagonist wakes up and finds they have become a giant.

    b. Protagonist goes over to best friend's house. Best friend has turned into an octopus.

    c.

    d.

    e.

    f.

    g.

    h.

    i.

    j.

    2. Choose one transformation from your list. Write a story where this transformation changes the household/relationship/family.

    3. Protagonist tries to change the situation. Write three separate instances of them trying to change the situation.

    4. Protagonist renounces trying to change things. What must they give up?

    5. Do NOT fix the situation or make things ok for the protagonist, but at the same time indicate, how they have possibly grown as people through the experience.

    Note: this is not an easy exercise to do. But it is an important one in that it enables us to see how we might be making our other stories "all right" too fast. And it frees us to write sad stories. So much of life is sad, and stories can and ought to reflect this. In so doing stories can also give us ways to understand and deal with our sadness.

That's why we read and that's why we write -- to give voice to difficult emotions and circumstances. This is perhaps the greatest gift that Magical Realism offers.

By way of the unreal, we can access complex emotional states that we cannot approach in any other way.

Speaking of which...

B. The ending as a hall of mirrors: Magical Realism and metafiction.

Some magical realist narratives blow our minds by going beyond any sort of expected ending, and in fact, refuse to "end" at all. Márquez's *100 Years of Solitude* does exactly this. Despite the fact that it's filled with many sad occurrences, the book ends or rather stops, in a very surprising, alienating way. The final character named Aureliano (there have been several) discovers -- in the very last pages of the novel -- a book of predictions setting out the entire story that we have just read. This move is a metafictional maneuver. Metafiction is a type of fiction that calls attention to its fictionality and comments in some way upon itself. In this way, Márquez's novel turns in on itself, like a snake eating its own tail. It also turns outward; it is a story about a story about a story about a story, as though we were standing in a room with mirrors on all sides, seeing ourselves reflected infinitely. Our sadness about the destruction of the Buendía family is assuaged (or is it?) by our wonder at the magic of storytelling, a magic which is endless.

Writing Exercise in Metafiction.

Take a story that you have already written. Instead of the ending you have, try substituting:

- A TV show
- A movie
- A YouTube video
- A podcast
- A graphic novel or zine
- Any narrative art form you like (a dance, a song, a play)

In your closing paragraph, describe how what has just happened to the protagonist(s) is the subject of the story in this other piece of art.

Notice how the feeling of your piece changes. You can use this new ending as a replacement or as a jumping off point for re-thinking how you might want to "loosen up" your ending. You "might" even decide that you would like to seed this metafictional object somewhere earlier in the story, and then have it sprout and blossom at the end. Whatever you decide, this process will help your story feel more alive.

C. The ending as an opportunity for reflection: Magical Realism and the contemplative

In her remarkable essay "Our Stories, Ourselves: storytelling from East to West," Marie Mitsuke Moffatt notices that Japanese fairy tales often end with the protagonist alone contemplating a memory of a beautiful image. Appropriately, Japanese author Haruki Murakami's ends his novel *The Wind-Up Bird Chronicles* in a similar fashion. Toru, the protagonist quietly waits alone at the end of the novel, hoping that his wife will return and holding an image in his mind of his friend May wearing her blue hat on the bus. Aimee Bender's novel *The Particular Sadness of Lemon Cake* does something very similar with its ending, and the sudden appearance of a stranger adds to the power of the scene. Here is a quote from the end of the book:

> How once in junior high, I'd been caught actually kneeling in front of a vending machine, in prayer position, with bowed head, breathing a thank you into the little metallic grate that received the baggies after they fell down the chute? The security cop, touring the school, had laughed at me. I thought I liked Oreos, he chuckled. I love them, I told him solemnly, gripping the bag. I am in love with them, I said. (Aimee Bender, *The Particular Sadness of Lemon Cake*)

At the end of both these novels, we are asked to think outside of ourselves, to become quiet, and to contemplate the beauty and mystery of the world that surrounds us. That world can include the miraculous quality of the public school vending machine. I do a variation on contemplation at the end of my novel *The Puppet Turners of Narrow Interior*. Rather than giving

Henry Holbein exactly what he wants, I put him to work fixing a fence that he once played upon as a child as he contemplates his (possible) Jewish identity.

Writing Exercises with Contemplation.

Take a story that you have already written and substitute one of the following for the ending that you have:

1. Take a happy ending that feels too simple or too easy, and substitute a paragraph where the protagonist is alone at the end of the story in a beautiful place where he or she can wonder at the natural surroundings.

2. Take either a happy or sad ending and change it by putting your protagonist in a place where he or she can look at a beautiful object. This could be a department store, a museum, or someone one's house. End your story with a description of this beautiful thing. This beautiful thing can be something very small and everyday.
   Make your protagonist be alone. Then, if it feels right, add one more (and only one more person) to the scene.
   3. Get to work. Instead of a happy ending, put your protagonist to work, doing something mundane but useful.

4. Go big. What about choosing your favorite two possible endings and using them both? Or even give us three. John Fowles offers his readers three different endings in his 1969 novel *The French Lieutenant's Woman.*

Experiment with these endings. You may decide that you want to keep your new paragraph AND your old ending, and that you'd like to mesh them somehow -- having the moment of contemplation precede or come after the happy/sad ending. Or you may realize that your story IS about contemplation, and you will see your story in a new light and with new emotions.

In writing Magical Realism we have the room to be very funny or very sad or something -- many things -- in between. As you work with this kind of writing you can explore ways to incorporate both laughter and tears in your writing, as well as express other kinds of emotions -- longing, jealousy, admiration, wonder -- that will take on a new luster because they are being treated as special, magical, and deliciously strange.

9. And Now the Big Question: <u>Why</u> Magical Realism?

What we care about in our society/world and the issues that we don't understand are the very things that we want and need to write about. But getting at these questions in a non-judgmental and non-clichéd way is hard for most writers. Since these questions are BIG questions, it can be difficult for us to address these matters with an open mind and from a fresh point of view. What we "think" is right may blind us to our own preconceived biases and prejudices. The more strongly we feel, the harder it can be to write about an issue in a nuanced and interesting way.

This is where Magical Realism comes in and can really help us do powerful things as writers.

In his short story "CivilWarLand in Bad Decline," George Saunders tells a story about a soon to go bankrupt theme park. This choice of subject matter -- along with the implication that the protagonist and his associates are all white -- immediately plunges an American reader into a complex and painful space by asking us to think about the extent to which popular history has effectively white-washed our country's traumatic civil war, and also to think about how American consumerism (or is it capitalism?) has relegated this crucial turning point into a dumbed-down money maker.

But equally important is the fact that this choice of approach forces Saunders himself to think and write differently about the topic. As a middle-class white male writer, he could easily fall into all number of easy responses to Civil War history. But the extremity of the story forces its protagonist -- and its creator -- to think differently about it.

Likewise, in *Pedro Páramo*, Juan Rulfo uses conversations among the dead to give us a troubled, uncomfortable picture of the confused nature of the Mexican Revolution. Has it been successful? If so, what's going on with this deserted town where dead people talk about social inequality and personal horror? Juan Rulfo surely had his own very personal responses to the Mexican Revolution and to Mexican history as a whole. But the cacophony of voices speaking from the grave complicates whatever his own personal point of view may have been.

There are other examples of how Magical Realism forces writers to go into scary places and come up with surprising answers that just open up more questions. Haruki Murakami uses *The Wind-Up Bird Chronicle* to gesture towards the Japanese atrocities in Nanjing and the rage that Chinese and Mongolian peoples feel towards Japan. In "Skinless," Aimee Bender has two characters -- a Jewish social worker and a troubled Neo Nazi -- join in an erotic and possibly fatal encounter. Will they both survive it? What will happen next?

In other words, Magical Realist fiction leads -- just about always -- in a political and ethically questioning direction. Note, though, that these writers are not making a political speech, or attempting to cram a message -- religious, political, legal or what have you -- down the throat of the reader. They are using magical realism to ask questions about who we are and what we value, and -- equally important -- what the hidden assumptions and problems might be in those values that we hold. They are not writing propaganda, but art. Propaganda shuts down thinking. Literary art asks you what you think and how what you're thinking might need to go further and wider. Which is why we need it and love it.

Let's play with these ideas.

A. Make a list of the political/social/ethical issues you care about most.
1. Example (gun safety)
2.
3.
4.
5.
6.
7.
8.
9.
10.

B. Now imagine a school, town, state, or country where the thing that is the OPPOSITE of what you believe in happens on a daily basis.

1. Example (a town where students are asked to murder their parents in order to vent their rage about their future and they in turn get shot by their teachers to control population)*

2.
3.
4.
5.
6.
7.
8.
9.
10.

C. Look back at your second list. Try writing a fairy tale like story about one or more of these items.

D. Then experiment with your story, using some of the techniques offered in earlier chapters.

I'm guessing your story will be pretty interesting. It may make you a bit uncomfortable. But that's ok.

Asking difficult questions about our society and world is also part of what Magical Realism does.

May you continue to ask hard questions in your writing.

----

    *My story "Guilty Creatures" (*Bacopa Review*, 2012) works on the basis of the example that I gave. It's a pretty good story, although it's sad.

10. Books and Articles Mentioned in this Book as well as a few more Reading Selections

Magical Realist novels and story collections mentioned in this book

Kathleen Alcalá, *Spirits of the Ordinary*
Andre Alexis, *Fifteen Dogs*
Ryka Aoki, *He Mele a Hilo*
Aimee Bender, *The Girl in the Flammable Skirt*
Includes the stories "The Rememberer,"
"Skinless," and "Marzipan"
The Particular Sadness of Lemon Cake
Roberto Bolaño, *Nazi Literature in the Americas*
Mikhail Bulgakov, *The Master and Margarita*
Robert Olen Butler, "Jealous Husband Returns in Form of Parrot"
Italo Calvino, *Cosmicomics*
Sesshu Foster, *Atomic Aztex*
Heather Fowler, *Beautiful Ape Girl Baby*
John Fowles, *The French Lieutenant's Woman*
Stephanie Barbé Hammer, *The Puppet Turners of Narrow Interior*
Kazuo Ishiguro, *Never Let Me Go* (More speculative than MR but notable for its use of language)
Eugene Ionesco, *The Bald Soprano*
Franz Kafka, *The Metamorphosis,*
"Poseidon"
Niko Kazantzakis, *The Last Temptation of Christ*
Alain Mabanckou, *Memoirs of a Porcupine*

Gabriel García Márquez, *100 Years of Solitude*
"The Handsomest Drowned Man in the World"
Toni Morrison, *Beloved*
Haruki Murakami, *The Wind-Up Bird Chronicle*
Ben Okri, *The Famished Road*
Ovid. *The Metamorphoses*
Juan Rulfo, *Pedro Paramo*
Leslie Marmon Silko, *Ceremony.*
George Saunders, *CivilWarLand in Bad Decline.*
Pastoralia. Includes the story "Sea Oak"
"Semplica-Girl Diary"
Patrick Süskind, *Perfume*
B. Traven, *The Night Visitor and Other Stories*
Jeanette Winterson, *Sexing the Cherry*
Mo Yan, *Life and Death are Wearing Me Out*

Writers on Magical Realism, Fairy Tales and other Genres and Techniques referred to and cited in this book

Aimee Bender, "Why the Best Way to Get Creative is to Make Some Rules." *O, the Oprah Magazine*. July 2012.
http://www.oprah.com/spirit/writing-every-day-writers-rules-aimee-bender#ixzz4BWYz7EJj
Zoe Brooks, *Reviews of Magic Realism Books and More.* https://magic-realism-books.blogspot.com/
Changing Minds, "Vladimir Propp's Narrateemes."

http://changingminds.org/disciplines/storytelling/plots/propp/31_narratemes.htm_

Emory University, "Magical Realism" https://scholarblogs.emory.edu/postcolonialstudies/2014/06/21/magical-realism/

Erin Martinsen, "Breaking down Cinderella" https://emartinsen.wordpress.com/2011/10/17/breaking-down-cinderella/

Marie Mitsuke Mockett, "Our Stories, Our Selves: Storytelling from East to West." January 2016. http://lithub.com/our-fairy-tales-ourselves-storytelling-from-east-to-west/

Vladimir Propp, *Morphology of the Russian Folktale*.

Pursed Lip Square Jaw. Games and quizzes, http://www.purselipsquarejaw.org/surrealist_games/.

Bruce Holland Rogers, "What is Magical Realism, Really?" 2002, http://www.writing-world.com/sf/realism.shtml

David Young, and Keith Hollaman, ed, *Magical Realist Fiction: An Anthology*.

Lois Parkinson Zamora and Wendy B. Farris, ed, *Magical Realism: Theory, History, Community.*

Some classics any magical realism fan needs to know

Hans Christian Andersen. *Fairy Tales and Stories*. Includes the "Little Mermaid."

The Brothers Grimm. *Fairy Tales.*

ETA Hoffmann, *Collected Fairy Tales.*

Robert Louis Stevenson, *The Strange Case of Dr. Jekyll and Mr. Hyde.*

Gabrielle-Suzanne Barbot de Villeneuve, *Beauty and the Beast.*

Oscar Wilde, *A Picture of Dorian Gray.*

Some inspiring non-literary Magical Realist narratives

Graphic novels
Neil Gaiman, *The Sandman* series

Art Spiegelman, *MAUS 1 and 2* (graphic "novel" -- technically non-fiction)

Noelle Stevenson, *Nimona.*

Film
Amélie (dir. Jean-Pierre Jennet [original French title is *Le fabuleux destin d'Amélie Poulain]*)

Being John Malkowich (dir. Spike Jonze)

Lady in the Water (dir. M. Night Shyamalan)

Orpheus (dir. Jean Cocteau)

Pan's Labyrinth (dir. Guillermo del Toro [original Spanish title is *el laberinto del fauno*])

Television
Dead Like Me (tv show, creator, Bryan Fuller)

Pushing Daisies (tv show, creator, Bryan Fuller)

11. Bonus Chapter: Mind-Boggling Games and Six More Prompts

A. Games: Here are a few questions taken and adapted from a quiz generated by the wonderful folks at purse lips square jaw.

1. SCOREBOARD. Rate the following:
(+20 = unreserved approval, 0 = utter indifference, -20 = total abomination)

Irrationality
Humor
Civilization
Desire
Honesty
Religion
Madness
Logic
Happiness
Weakness

2. A FANCIFUL QUESTION:
If you saw in a cafe, reunited, everyone with whom you have been sexually involved, and the one you love standing there alone, what would you do? Write a short scene.

3. EXPERIMENTS WITH OBJECTS
Answer the following questions about artichoke:
Is it diurnal or nocturnal?

What illness does it call to mind?

In what city does it live?

Is it happy or unhappy?

What might its profession be?

Is it capable of metamorphosis?

How does it get around?

With what historical figure can it be associated?

How would you kill it?

What scent goes with it?

Is it favorable to love?

What is its favorite song?

4. CERTAIN POSSIBILITIES RELATING TO THE IRRATIONAL EMBELLISHMENT OF A CITY

How would you conserve, displace, modify, transform, or suppress certain aspects of your city?

Example: New York City: The Statue of Liberty
Paint it pink. Then green. Then make it invisible.

5. WOULD YOU OPEN THE DOOR?

There is a knock at the door. You open it and see Emma Goldman. Would you invite her in (and why)? Or close the door (and why)? If you don't know who Emma Goldman is, look her up, change her identity in 3 ways, and proceed. Write a paragraph.

6. CREATING NEW SUPERSTITIONS

Come up with a new superstition.

Example: When passing a fire station, take off your

glasses and spin around 3 times. Then go to your nearest taco stand. Order orange juice.

7. CHANGING THE LAWS OF SCIENCE
What 5 new rules of nature would you like to propose? Example: rain falls up from the ground not down from the sky.

Choose 1-3 of these and write a story from the point of view of the person who discovers these new laws.

8. ALTERING THE EQUIPMENT
"Can one modify the human?" asks Jean Rostand. Does a modification of our equipment seem useful? Desirable? Give 4 suggestions.

Take a look at what you've written. Choose 2 of these and try writing a story based on what you've come up with.

B. Here are 6 more prompts (more, if you do all the options)

1. History exercise. List 7 battles or wars or natural catastrophes that interest you. If you like do some research online or at the library.
   1. The eruption of Vesuvius
   2. The Battle of Little Bighorn
   3.
   4.

5.

6.

7.

Now, design a theme park around this battle or natural catastrophe. Who might work there? Doing what? Who's the supervisor? What's for sale at the gift shop? What kinds of snacks are offered? What ghosts might haunt such a theme park?

What kinds of professional conflicts might arise between the workers and management?

That's your story.

2. Return of the Living Dead.

What relative/friend do you and/or your family **wish** would come back from the dead? What unforeseen problems might develop if they did come back? What would they want? What room would they stay in? What positive outcomes might occur?

That's your story.

3. Weird (computer) Science (especially great if you are NOT scientifically inclined)

Look through a kid's chemistry biology textbook (or website) or look through the WIRED archives and make up 10 discoveries/inventions that your protagonist invents/ buys/ encounters.

1. (Example) Iphone app that senses your emotions and sends them to EVERYONE on your contact list (including doctors, dentists, and ex-lovers).

2. (Example) Language teaching app in the language lab at school that decides to make up its own language and teach everyone in the school that language instead of Spanish, Arabic, Chinese etc.

    3.
    4.
    5.
    6.
    7.
    8.
    9.
    10.

4. Mixed Vegetables. Try using 2 of these plot devices in tandem with each other.

5. Strange and not glamorous super-powers. List 10 inconvenient magical or super powers that a person/family/group of friends/town/country might have. (This is the basis for Aimee Bender's novel *The Particular Sadness of Lemon Cake*).

    1. (Example) The ability to hear plants and trees growing (and dying).

    2.
    3.
    4.
    5.
    6.
    7.
    8.

9.

10.

How does your protagonist discover their super-power? Who else in the family -- if anyone -- has a similar or analogous power? How do they learn to manage/control it? Or do they? What mistakes do they make? What price do they pay? Whom do they tell? Who do they love? Who loves them?

6. Your secret hobby/obsession as a fake encyclopedia. Most of us have at least one hobby/obsession. What's yours? List some of your noble and less noble obsessions.

    1. Example -- chocolate
    2. Example -- knitting
    3.
    4.
    5.
    6.
    7.
    8.
    9.
    10.

Now craft a story composed of encyclopedia entries of the most beloved aspects of this hobby. Who discovered knitting anyway? Don't tell the truth. Make up a story for its history. Think this can't work? Think again. An unhealthy obsession forms the basis of

Bolaño's mind-boggling fictional encyclopedia, *Nazi Literature in the Americas*.

Appendix A: How to Freewrite

Freewriting is a creative writing technique that is used the world over to free up your imagination and get the writing juices flowing.

The following excerpt is drawn from an essay by Peter Elbow, an American teacher and writer, who is famous for developing the use of this writing tool.

From FREEWRITING by Peter Elbow (Writing Without Teachers, Harvard UP, 1973) link to full essay: http://faculty.buffalostate.edu/wahlstrl/eng309/Freewriting.pdf

Rules for Freewriting

- • Do free writing exercises **at least three times a week.**
- • The idea is simply to write for ten minutes (later on, perhaps fifteen or twenty).
- • Don't stop for anything. Go quickly without rushing.
- • Never stop to look back, to cross something out, to wonder how to spell something, to wonder what word or thought to use, or to think about what you are doing.

• • If you can't think of a
word or a spelling, just use a
squiggle or else write "I can't
think what to say, I can't think
what to say" as many times as
you want; or repeat the last
word you wrote over and over
again; or anything else.

Here is an example of a fairly
coherent exercise (sometimes they are
very incoherent, which is fine):

I think I'll write what's on my
mind, but the only thing on my mind
right now is what to write for ten
minutes. I've never done this before
and I'm not prepared in any way--the
sky is cloudy today, how's that? Now
I'm afraid I won't be able to think
of what to write when I get to the
end of the sentence--well, here I am
at the end of the sentence--here I am
again, again, again, again, at least
I'm still writing--Now I ask is there
some reason to be happy that I'm
still writing--ah yes! Here comes the
question again--What am I getting out
of this? What point is there in it?
It's almost obscene to always ask it

but I seem to question everything that way and I was gonna say something else pertaining to that but I got so busy writing down the first part that I forgot what I was leading into. This is kind of fun oh don't stop writing--cars and trucks speeding by somewhere out the window, pens clittering across peoples' papers. The sky is still cloudy--is it symbolic that I should be mentioning it? Huh? I dunno. Maybe I should try colors, blue, red, dirty words--wait a minute--no can't do that, orange, yellow, arm tired, green pink violet magenta lavender red brown black green--now I can't think of any more colors--just about done--relief? Maybe.

Freewriting may seem crazy but actually it makes simple sense.
Almost everyone interposes a massive and complicated series of editings between the time the words start to be born into consciousness and when they finally come of the end of the pencil or typewriter onto the page. **This is partly because**

schooling **makes us obsessed with the** "mistakes" **we make in writing.**

But it's not just "mistakes" or "bad writing" we edit as we write. **We also edit unacceptable thoughts and feelings, as we do in speaking.**

Editing, in itself, is not the problem. Editing is usually necessary if we want to end up with something satisfactory. **The problem is that editing goes on at the same time as producing. . . . Practiced regularly, free writing undoes the ingrained habit of editing at the same time you are trying to produce. It will make writing less blocked because words will come more easily** . . ..

Next time you write, notice how often you stop yourself from writing down something you were going to write down. Or else cross it out after it's been written. "Naturally," you say, "it wasn't any good." But think for a moment about the occasions when you spoke well. Seldom was it because you first got the beginning right. Usually it was a

94

matter of a halting or even a garbled beginning, but you kept going and your speech finally became coherent and even powerful. There is a lesson here for writing: trying to get the beginning just right is a formula for failure--and probably a secret tactic to make yourself give up writing. **Make some words, whatever they are, and then grab hold of that line and reel in as hard as you can.** Afterwards you can throw away lousy beginnings and make new ones. This is the quickest way to get into good writing.

The habit of compulsive, premature editing doesn't just make writing hard. It also makes writing dead. Your voice is damped out by all the interruptions, changes, and hesitations between the consciousness and the page. **In your natural way of producing words there is a sound, a texture, a rhythm--a voice--which is the main source of power in your writing.** I don't know how it works, but this voice is the force that will make a reader listen to you. **Maybe you don't like your voice; maybe**

people have made fun of it. But it's the only voice you've got. It's your only source of power. If you keep writing in it, it may change into something you like better. But if you abandon it, you'll likely never have voice and never be heard.

===

Some freewriting exercises that I like to do:

1. Set a timer for 2 minutes. Write about how you are feeling RIGHT NOW. Describe your mood, physical sensations, and anything else that comes to mind.

2. Set a timer for 5 minutes. Start with what you remember about when you woke up this morning. Then let your mind wander.

3. Sense exercises: Set your timer for 10 minutes:

a) Look at something or someone. Describe them exhaustively, til your mind wanders.

b) What's that sound? Describe it -- if sound had a shape or a smell or a color what would it be?

c) Junk drawer -- reach to the back of your junk drawer. Describe what you feel.

d) Blind refrigerator -- close your eyes or have someone help you, smell one thing in your fridge.

Appendix B: Lingo Lists

For fairy tale vocabulary:
https://myvocabulary.com/word-list/fantasy-and-imagination-vocabulary/

Astronaut vocabulary:
http://astropuppiesinspace.com/vocabulary.htm

For robotics:
http://www.motoman.com/glossary.php.

For cowboy lingo:
http://www.lrgaf.org/guide/western-cowboy.htm

Postscript: Before we go...

List 10 topics, issues, interests and/or people you would write a story about if you think you had enough time, talent, skills, knowledge, and/or courage:

1.
2.
3.
4.
5.
6.
7.
8.
9.
10.

Now write the 3 different opening sentences based on 3 of the items on your list:

1.
2.
3.

Pick one, and write the story. You can do it!

About the Author

Stephanie Barbé Hammer is a 5-time nominee for the Pushcart Prize in fiction, nonfiction, and poetry. She has published work in *The Bellevue Literary Review*, *Pearl*, *the James Franco Review*, and the *Hayden's Ferry Review* among other places. She is the author of the prose poem chapbook *Sex with Buildings* (Dancing Girl Press), a full-length poetry collection, *How Formal?* (Spout Hill Press), and a magical realist novel, *The Puppet Turners of Narrow Interior* (Urban Farmhouse Press).

A former New Yorker, Stephanie now lives in Coupeville WA with interfaith blogger/author Larry Behrendt. She is currently working on a poetry collection about a relentless urbanite navigating a rural habitat, a novella about a Beverly Hills teenager who wants to be a plumber, and a novel about two mixed up women with magical powers searching for a missing person on a vintage train bound for Montreal.

About the Series

As actual charcoal provides the artist with a simple, elegant means with which to bring their vision to the canvas, Spout Hill's Charcoal Series of books aims to give writers concise and clear access to the tools needed to meet their academic and creative writing needs. We hope these guides, published in collaboration with leading authors and educators, will serve writers of all ages in perfecting and honing their craft.